SILENCE UTTERED

SILENCE UTTERED

A TALE OF UNITY

First Edition

Catherine Klinger

SECRETS-OF-LIFE
PUBLISHING

Secrets-of-Life Publishing

550 Okeechobee Blvd. – Suite 1519

West Palm Beach, FL 33401-6340 U.S.A.

www.silenceuttered.com

Copyright © 2014 by Catherine Albrecht Klinger

First edition

All rights reserved.
No part of this book may be reproduced or transmitted
in any form or by any means, electronic or mechanical,
including photocopying, recording, or by any information storage
and retrieval system, without written permission from the author,
except for the inclusion of brief quotations in a review.

ISBN 978-0-9914835-0-1

Library of Congress Control Number: 2014901827

Printed in the United States of America

Cover design by Robb Klinger

To every child in the world

who needs clean water

CONTENTS

PROLOGUE

    THE BEGINNING------------------------- 11

    THE FILE BOX -------------------------- 23

    THE GAME -------------------------------- 39

    REVOLUTION------------------------------ 55

    PARTNERS-------------------------------- 69

EPILOGUE

PROLOGUE

Walk into the forest

Come upon a brook

Listen to it babble

Like the verses in this book

Books and brooks are messengers

The Message has no name

Beyond all words and images

What's different is the same

THE BEGINNING

In the beginning
There were no words

No Rocks

No Trees

No Sky

No Birds

Nothing to see

Or be

Or do

No one to talk about

Or talk to

14 | Silence Uttered

But Silence uttered

Silence uttered ONEness

That's all it had to say

Out of nowhere suddenly

ONE formless lump of clay

ONEness was not happy

ONEness was not sad

Life could not have been described

As either good or bad

Love did not exist of course

But neither then did hate

"I agree with me," sighed ONE

"There's nothing to debate"

"I'm here

 I'm there

 I'm everywhere

 I'm everything," cried ONE

"It's not exactly boring, but

It's not exactly fun"

"I wonder what would happen if

I split myself in two

Variety could spice life up

And entertain me too"

"This change presents a problem

That really must be solved

Once the parts are separate

Why would they get involved?"

"I'll have to build the message in—

Design them with a clue—

Shape them so they'll interlock

They'll know just what to do"

Thus ONE began to chisel

To sculpt the perfect fit

Two jigsaw puzzle pieces

That could be merged or split. . .

The pieces started talking

They laughed and joked and played

ONEness was delighted with

The difference Twoness made

Twoness was delighted with

The thought of being ONE

"Me and You," said one of two

"Could have a lot of fun"

Silence uttered

Every time

Those jigsaw pieces

Merged

And that is how

The world was filled

With Rocks

And Trees

And Birds

THE FILE BOX

Rock sat down and sat and sat
Unmoved by this unmoved by that

Bird, in contrast, flew away

Sunrise lit the dawning Day

Rivers fed the Waterfall

Wind blew softly, Grass grew tall

Warm and pungent, lush and green

Calm, harmonious, pristine

Eventually, the discord came

Concocted by the human brain

A serpent by another name

Seeking fortune, seeking fame

Ego arrived to steal the wealth

Claiming the garden for himself

He frowned on Rock and Bird and Tree

"What good is all this Harmony?"

"These happy fools don't know what's wrong

That attitude won't last for long

Harmony is for the Birds

Egos have a need for Words"

"Words create duality

Objectify reality

Words cut up the Birds-eye view

Dividing me and we from you"

"A conqueror must first divide

Divisive Thoughts will be applied

When Differences are emphasized

They'll see the garden through my eyes"

"I'll segregate the Rocks from Trees

Make them think they're Enemies

To modify the Thoughts they think

I need the help of Pen and Ink"

"Let's build a box, a box of Words

Proper Nouns and 'To be' Verbs

Words that individualize

Stereotype and stigmatize"

"A File Box of Names and Places

Ages, Genders, severed Races

Everybody gets a niche

Poor can't mingle with the Rich"

"In The Box, there's a condition

'Live within your definition'

One file card per entity

Provides complete Identity"

"A card for Christian, one for Jew

Muslim, Buddhist, and Hindu

Separate cards for Sister, Brother

Pitting them against each other"

"The garden will be mine to seize

If I create some Hierarchies

Ranking them by Class and Caste

Guarantees some finish last"

"I'm always going to be the first

To quench my hunger and my thirst

I'll take it all and then take more

Exploiting's what an Ego's for"

"Greedy friends will hold top spots

Supervising the Have-nots

Sick? Weak? Homeless? Overpassed!

File the Desperate in the Trash"

"Once they know that Categories

Will determine their Life Stories

They'll succumb to Domination

Suffering Quiet Desperation"

"But Labeling is just the start

Of tearing garden roots apart

My monarchy will be complete

When I get subjects to compete"

"Watch and see me capitalize

While they are fighting for their lives

They're all boxed up; I've got their ear

To make them fight, I'll foster Fear"

"To foster Fear, I'll tell a lie:

Demand exceeds their scarce Supply

My ideal world Economy

Is based on Fear of Scarcity"

Ego declared a Reign of Greed

'Never Enough' conveyed his creed

His strategy could be defined

As 'Exploitative State of Mind'

Ego reigned and lines were crossed

Profit-making at any cost

Lives consumed by Acquisition

Fueled by vicious Competition

The Box was filled with Ego's rules

Lesson plans for all the schools

Exploitation caught on fast

Greed was popular at last

Keeping step with Ego's orders

Sets of nations with strong borders

Gathered up their hostile forces

Waging war for scarce resources

Killing those who can't be bought

Scorching Earth with battles fought

Not a drop was left to drink

Ego drove them to The Brink

Brinks are chinks in the flow of life

Openings that shed some Light

Fending off a grave attack

ONEness always has our back

At the Brink before the End

ONE engaged a trusted friend

Mirror made a fearless leap

Dropping into Ego's sleep

THE GAME

"Ego" said the Mirror

"It's time to play The Game

You'll see, despite appearances

What's different is the same"

"Give me your attention

And I'll tell you what to do

Take this ball and throw it out

I'll throw it back to you"

Opponents took positions

One here—the other there

One served in, the other out

The ball flew through the air

In and out and out and in

From Me to You to Me

Mirror was a perfect match

They played whole-heartedly

Neither one could make a point

Love-Love the final score

"Can't we play some other game?

I'm good at tug-of-war"

"I want to win, to dominate

To conquer with my might

This game is lame and you're to blame

I'm ready for a fight"

Mirror answered mindfully

"If war is what you choose

 You clearly think that winning means

Someone has to lose"

"Your File Box with its rusty Locks

Can be a dangerous toy

Need and Greed and Selfishness

Are costing you your Joy"

Ego heard a gasp for air

From somewhere deep within

The burden of his Selfishness

Was suffocating him

"My heart is detonating

With existential pain

I carved the world in pieces

For fortune and for fame"

"How can I end the suffering

If I am suffering too?

Mirror," Ego pleaded

"Please tell me what to do"

"Here's a way to play The Game

All by yourself instead

Of playing with opponents,"

The Mirror promptly said

"Place yourself both in and out

And in the middle too

Take the ball and throw it out

Then throw it back to you"

Dizzy with these twists and turns

An angry Ego said

"This game is so illogical

It's messing with my head!"

"What you're asking me to do

Simply can't be done

Can't you see I'll lose Myself?

This game cannot be won"

"You think too hard," said Mirror

"If thinking's all you do

You'll never find the joy in life

That lies in wait for you"

"It takes a choice, a leap of faith

To find joy in your heart

Be guided by your inner voice

Reflection is an art"

"Reflect," continued Mirror

"The Other Side is you

Shift yourself from here to there

By changing points of view"

"When you're looking out your eyes

The outside's what you see

Look in *and* out and live your life

With true Integrity"

Thus Ego looked inside and out

Looked ONEness in the eye

And—after much reflection—said

"I think You must be I"

The purpose of this insight

Was now quite plain to see

Ego took his journey

To find The Golden Key

"Empathy's The Golden Key

For a change in our direction

It frees us from the biases

That block our Reconnection"

"Before I saw Myself in You

I lived my life alone

The Game has turned me inside out

And paved my way back Home"

REVOLUTION

A turning point, a nexus
In the flow of evolution
Ego awoke and set the stage
For heart-felt Revolution

Revolving through the garden
He twirled The Golden Key
"I played a game that changed my mind
About Reality"

"Until I turned myself around

I wanted to be King

I boxed you up divisively

Polluting everything"

"The Golden Key of Empathy

Unlocks my Box of Lies

And liberates us from the Masks

That hide us in disguise"

"When I played The Mirror's Game
I got a chance to see
That who we always really are
Transcends Identity"

"Identity is foreground
Mere images we're seeing
Connectedness lies deep within
The essence of our being"

"Beyond the things we think we are

Beyond what we can name

Beyond all words and images

What's different is the same"

"We are different *and* the same

It's time to spread the word

On the outside, we are different

A Rock is not a Bird"

"Variety's the spice of life

What's different makes life fun

If only we'd remember

We started out as ONE"

"On the inside, we are Family

ONE constant common core

The Mission that unites us

Calls for The End of War"

"Join me in Revolution

My turnaround's a start

Everyone can make the shift

To living heart-to-heart"

The strength of their Compassion

Unfastened rusty Locks

Collectively, they overthrew

The old and musty Box

Chains of Thought fell to the ground

Forever bent and broken

Silence uttered in their hearts

When Words of Love were spoken

Flourishing as kindred souls

In jubilant rebirth

They saw themselves as gardeners

Sustainers of The Earth

Gratitude produced a stream

Of giving everywhere

Water flowed abundantly

To each an equal share

Sunshine filled the garden

With vital Energy

Fueling the beginning of

A new Economy

Scarcity ran out the gate

Once old rules were discarded

Fear ran too, along with Hate

"Let's get the party started"

"A party, yes, we'll throw a ball"

Said Bird to Rock and Tree

"Tonight's the night to celebrate

Divine Diversity"

Bird tweeted near and tweeted far:

TONIGHT COME ONE, COME ALL

RECONNECT, COME AS YOU ARE

COME TO THE PARTNERS BALL

PARTNERS

"It's Beginning now," said End
"Bring a Foe," insisted Friend
Out stepped In the ballroom door
Length chased Width across the floor

Fast relaxed and danced with Slow
Maybe danced with Yes and No
Dusk cut in on Day and Night
Gray cut in on Black and White

"Why be Average?" Low asked High

"Let's be Bold!" asserted Shy

"Let's be Happy," offered Sad

"Swing your partner, Good," said Bad

Networking throughout the night

"Nothing's Wrong," reported Right

"Nothing's missing," True told False

Partners joined in sultry waltz

Dinner bells began to chime

Fast and Slow got there on time

They all got there when they were able

Places for everyone at the table

Up sat Down, "It's time to eat"

Fat and Skinny shared a seat

Crazy settled next to Sane

"Fancy meal," requested Plain

"Don't be Sloppy," cautioned Neat

Bitter poured a drink for Sweet

All the Empty cups were Full

"There's a balance, Push" said Pull

"Add it up," advised Subtract

"Plus tells Minus how to act

It's a two-way interaction

Based on mutual attraction"

Simple smiled, "Life's Complex

She's Concave and He's Convex

Sometimes they're a perfect fit

Sometimes they can't wait to split"

"It's a puzzle, Lost then Found

"An enigma all around"

Silence laughed without a Sound

Superficial hugged Profound

"Take a Break," prescribed Repair

Hopefulness replaced Despair

Shallow dug down Deep inside

Narrow blossomed into Wide

Ordinary took the cue

"I'll be Special; you can too"

"I'll be Smoother now," said Rough

"I'll be Tender now," said Tough

"I'll be Quiet now," said Loud

"I'll be Humble now" said Proud

"I'll be Softer now," said Hard

"No one's Perfect," counseled Marred

"Thanks for shooting Straight," said Bent

"Things can Change," said Permanent

"Makes a Difference," Same replied

Lived agreed and quickly Died

Grieve shook hands with Celebrate

Early yawned, "It's getting Late"

Hot remarked, "It's getting Cold"

"Makes me tired, Young," said Old

Bottom looked around for Top

Off and On asked Start to Stop

To went From and Back went Forth

East drove West and South drove North

Right turned Left and Left turned Right

Dark turned off the ballroom Light

"Party's over Now," said Then

"Every night we'll dance again"

EPILOGUE

Deep asleep in dream tonight

As logic slips away

Find yourself remembering

The stillness of the clay

Make the reconnection

If you feel you are alone

In the still and silent space

All pathways lead to Home

Silence utters in our hearts

ONE simple Truth, unbroken

The Source remains Unthinkable

It's Whole and can't be spoken

Gratitude

Amazing people participated in the creation, design, and production of *Silence Uttered: A Tale of Unity*.

Robb Klinger designed the book cover. Zach English edited. Friends and colleagues offered support and recommended changes. In alphabetical order by first name, they included: Eva Hausman; K.C. Layfield; Karen Lauer; Katy Gilpatric; Lynne Tobin; Mary Mertz; Monica Goldberg; Nikki Kinkaide; Regina Grund; and Sandy Goldfarb. Ronald Gomez generated marketing ideas.

My father, John Albrecht, bought me my first typewriter. My mother, Virginia Albrecht, inspired me to write. My husband, Ron Klinger, provided technical expertise and partnered with me—as always—every step of the way.

Finally, I want to thank everyone who reads this book and shares its message with friends.

About water.org

Net proceeds from sales of this book are donated to water.org.

> Every 20 seconds, a child dies from a water-related disease.

"Water.org has a simple yet daunting mission—we want everyone in the world to be able to take a safe drink of water in our lifetime…We think about the one billion people who are living and dying for water access a bit differently than a traditional philanthropic approach—we see them as individuals with financial power, rights, responsibilities, and energy to design their own futures…"

- From *IN OUR LIFETIME: Deconstructing the Global Water Crisis and Securing Safe Water for All*
  Gary White and Matt Damon, Co-Founders

About the Author

Catherine Klinger ("Dr. K.") wrote the first chapter of this book while living without running water in a log cabin in the mountains of Idaho. At that time, everything she owned fit in a backpack.

Years later—committing to make the workplace more creative and inclusive—the author reentered the mainstream where she climbed Fortune 500 ladders. Her work with CEOs clarified some of the dilemmas examined in this book.

An advocate of spiritual leadership, Dr. K. currently serves on the faculty of a university in Florida. She lives in West Palm Beach with her husband, Ron, and their cat, Bella.

Go to www.silenceuttered.com for updates on the author's donations to water.org. She intends to raise ONE million dollars in her lifetime.

ORDER BOOKS

www.silenceuttered.com